CONTENTS

This book is dedicated to my three amazing daughters, Mahogany, Ashia and Mizan. I hope that the life I lead encourages you to be the very best person you came to this life to be. I wish for you the courage to live your dreams, no matter what.

Glimpse into my journey

Welcome to You're More Than Their Mother™: *RE*-claim, *RE*-align and *RE*-balance your life. This 'movement' started for me the moment I knew I was pregnant back in 1999. Honestly, none of my children were planned. Sure, I know what makes babies but I mean from a financial, educational and social responsibility level of planning. I have never been a girl that made any long term plans—things just seemed to work out the way I wanted and I situated my life around that type of haphazard living. Hey, if it wasn't broke---no need to fix it, right? While it was fun and I enjoyed many adventures, having my children made me realize the necessity of planning and purposed living. I created a legacy (in my children); I was a direct example, whether I wanted to be or not.

The truth is, I have always dreamed in color. I knew that I wanted lots of money, to travel the world, marry the man of my dreams and do be and have what I wanted…..in all of that I never imagined children. It took me a very long time to admit it, but my truth is: I didn't know I wanted children until they were born. I liked the idea of pregnancy……the attention, the pampering, the baby shower's, the foot rubs, etc., but beyond the novelty, I never gave it much thought. I was too focused on my dreams and this was an interruption to what I wanted. So I began my literal motherhood journey with the attitude that, "my children won't change me….I'm going to have what I want, I'll just have it with them". To think that I would be un-changed and wouldn't have to consider anything else was a bit naive. Well the short of the long story is, I quickly ended up frustrated, overweight, irritated and I was clueless as to how to move forward with my dreams as a mother. I didn't know what to do so I allowed myself to listen to the noise of society, old paradigms crept in, friends and family weighed in, and I began to live my life based on what others said I *should* be doing. Here are some of the mantras I used to live by: "It doesn't matter if I don't have...my children will....."; It's not about YOU, it's about those children....you don't matter; It doesn't matter what I look like, as long as my children are clean and looking good, etc. Those mantras became my philosophy and I began to conduct my life in such a way that not only neglected my person but it disregarded my spirit.

Fast forward to after the birth of my last child in 2004, there was a rumbling in my spirit that I could no longer ignore. I was morbidly obese, mildly depressed (self-diagnosed) and had a poor attitude; I wanted change. I didn't know what it was that I needed to do but I had to start somewhere. The thing that was most easily recognizable in me that needed change was my weight. For years I have gone up and down on the scale and for me it was always about vanity; I wanted to look good in my clothes and naked in the mirror. However, this time for me it was different. I wanted to not only look better but I wanted to feel better, so I set my intentions and began my journey. I started working out 5days a week—no matter what; from that I began to make better food choices; from that I began to read and research about the food I was putting in my body and healthy alternatives. Before I knew it I had lost 90+ pounds and began to look and feel better than I ever had in my life. In order for me to make those changes I had to make myself a priority. I had to give myself permission to walk away from some things and leave others undone because of greatest importance to me was to look and feel better. Sometimes the dishes went undone, the laundry had to wait, the children's hair-do had to last an 'extra' day; whatever, I needed to balance out all of our well-being. One of the biggest lessons I learned during that time was that everybody was ok with me not being around all the time---nobody died and truth be told, nobody even complained. I was the one holding MYSELF hostage to what I thought I should be doing opposed to what I wanted to do.

Needless to say, loosing weight, overcoming depression, eradicating self-sabotaging behaviors, improved attitude, etc continues to improve the quality of my life and motivate me to move. Now, I get to live my life in absolute FREEDOM of anyone else's ideals of who they want me to be and that includes my children (take a deep breath…..it's ok)!

Once I "stabilized" my physical, spiritual and emotional well-being my life began to RE-open up to me. I began to *RE*-call, in even more specific detail, some of the dreams I used to have when I was younger. I still wanted those things---I still had many goals I wanted to achieve. So I began to pray for guidance. I began to pray for alignment with the right people. I began to pray for discernment and wisdom. I had no idea how to go about getting anything I wanted, all I knew is that I was ready to do whatever it took to get me on the path to reaching my goals. Please note, while all of this was going on I *still* had to mother my children, be a wife to my husband, a daughter to my parents, etc. Life gave me no time-outs to allow me to figure things out or get myself together. I simply made the decision to do the best I could with what I had, every day. I made a concerted effort to take notice of what was happening in my life. I knew what I was learning would be of great benefit to my children and would possibly help them to learn, earlier, what had taken me all these years to learn.

In taking notice to what I was learning, reaping the benefits and sharing my story, I began to learn that many women had a story similar to mine. They were caught in the story of "just being a mother" and were unhappy with where they were in their personal lives. Well something struck me, I have always enjoyed speaking in front of audiences and I love sharing what I learn (I used to think I wanted to be a teacher). I thought, perhaps I could create a platform for sharing what I have learned with other moms. I held on to that idea for a while, but nothing ever came of it, or so I thought. One day, 'out of the blue' my aunt asked me to speak with a group of women at her church. She told me that I was an inspiration in how I was living my life and that these women could benefit from hearing my story and sharing what I have learned. I happily accepted with no expectations outside of that. The feedback was very positive and my story resonated with many of the women in the audience---I was just happy that I could be of service, never really thinking beyond that moment. As time went on, I was asked to speak at different schools, churches, organizations, and colleges. When the speaking engagements began to increase, I started to recognize just how much I LOVED being a speaker. I loved being transparent---sharing my life with people and putting the lessons that I learned in tangible steps so they could see themselves fulfill their purpose and follow their bliss. During this time I realized that I needed to monetize my gift. I knew that I was a gifted speaker and a motivated leader and I wanted to find a way to make money doing what I love (*RE*-claiming my original dream). That's when my prayers begin to shift. I began to get more specific with my request. I asked to be aligned with someone who could assist me in creating a repeatable, sustainable, residual business that would allow me to teach what I learned to women all over the world; to empower mothers to live their best life and to show them how to do it.

In the midst of all of this, I became a better person, mother, wife, daughter, etc. As I nurtured my desires, it lead me to become the absolute best expression of who I came to this planet to be, in all of my roles. What I learned, I began to practice and that automatically taught my children how to live their best life. They were experiencing the growth as it was happening. I made it a point to share with them every step of my journey (as I continue to) and why it is important to work hard, follow their dreams and never give up. I wanted them to know that my commitment to them was unrelenting and that choosing to love myself and doing some of what I wanted to do did not neglect the love I had for them. Conversely, it was teaching them the importance of loving themselves first in order to be of service to anyone else in the world.

So here I am, 13 years after the birth of my first child, saying loud and proud, I AM MORE THAN THEIR MOTHER. A statement that I feared saying out loud for many years because I feared others judgment, scrutiny and reprimand. Who knew that it would be the same statement that liberated me from the opinions of others and put me on the path of Empowerment, Entrepreneurship and Purpose.

You *ALWAYS* have a choice

How often do you feel overwhelmed, downtrodden and defeated? Have you ever felt that your desires don't matter and the needs of your children are more important, so why bother? If you're like me and thousands if not millions of other women, at some point in time the answer to at least one of those questions was a resounding, YES! Although we give it different adjectives to make it more universally understood, "stuck in a rut, overworked, under-appreciated, out of gas, etc.," the truth is it all means the same thing.

Let me serve as a reminder to something you already know but have likely forgotten: YOU HAVE A CHOICE in what you do, how you act and what you feel. All of the above mentioned are symptoms of a larger issue. Those words are your personal triggers that act as a coping mechanism that sends you into self-preservation mode and provokes others (those around you) to begin to sympathize and support you (because we usually don't just ask for help). At some point you bought into the 'lie' that you should be this "certain type" of mom, wife, daughter, etc. and are literally killing yourself trying to uphold those standards. You may have been subjected to the standards of your parents and their opinions when you were a child, but as an adult you have a choice and the freedom to use it. I often tell my audiences this, "a phenomena is nothing but a mass of people agreeing to accept a behavior, idea, or trend either verbally or non-verbally, and we accepted it ...... it doesn't make it right or even the best thing to do". Along the way, you fell into that phenomena of parenting. You just begin to follow these un-written rules and out of habit you begin to incorporate them into your life. Consider this, you're a person and you have the same ability as anyone else to create whatever you want. What if you started a new 'agreement' (phenomena)? Somebody else did it...why can't you? I know that it all sounds easier said than done. However, it doesn't make it any less necessary if you want to change how you are feeling and create a different experience than the one you are currently having. Take back your power—choose to feel differently no matter who stands in agreement with you! Always remember, you only need one agreement and that would be the one between you and your higher power.

Here's the truth:

- YOU are choosing to overwork yourself.
- YOU are choosing to be overwhelmed.
- YOU are choosing to not make what you want/your feelings a priority.

There is a way to balance it all. It is your JOB (and a gift to yourself) to figure out how. Do you realize that the way you are treating yourself is the way you are teaching your children to treat themselves (harsh but true)? When they see you constantly denying yourself the essentials you need to be happy, nurtured and refueled, they automatically think this is what they need to do (most times as a parent) and they duplicate the same behavior. Not because this is what you told them to do—rather, it is what they saw you do.

Are you wondering why others are treating you with disrespect, disregard or in-difference? Could it be that the treatment that you are receiving is a direct reflection of how you are treating yourself? Life only mirrors back what you put out. How you treat yourself will almost always be the way others treat you, plain and simple.

So while there is no blame, to you or anyone else, it is time for you to do better. Take time for yourself. Make yourself a priority. Teach your children how to take care of themselves by your actions, words don't teach. They need to know that taking a 'time out' is a good thing, we all have to refuel.

Go to the beach. Read a book. Watch TV. Sit outside. Do what you enjoy doing all while choosing not to feel guilty or provide explanation to anyone about why you are doing 'it'. So often, we cancel out our renewal moments with that of guilt and worry. You are so concerned with what others will think of you for taking time away for yourself, or you are thinking about other things that you could be doing, or you're un-easy because you believe you'll be set back from the next thing (for taking some time away); when in actuality that is all a myth that you chose to create and believe. All of those mental (sub-conscious) choices are debilitating and only keep you in self-limiting behavior and away from the thing you need most and that is some plain ol' RnR (rest and relaxation). Remember, if you are taken care of --- everybody you take care of will be better.

What's really bothering you?

Like everybody else in the world we have our ups and downs. Some days we are feeling good, other days---not so much. No explanation, we just can't seem to get out of our funk. Now before this goes any further, I want to be clear that I certainly understand that there are medical explanations for some of our mental conditions, chemical imbalances and neurological processes. However, I am talking about those days (or maybe even weeks) where you feel just, BLAH! Before you think the worse or label it depression I suggest that you use this time to run what I call a self-audit. Self-audits are a personal evaluation of your physical, spiritual and emotional well-being. It's a way to 'check-in' with yourself on how you are feeling and determine if the choices you are making are in support of your overall goal. Self- audits are a great way to clearly identify the "real" issue you are facing, reclaim your power over it and make a plan to come out of it.

As moms, we always seem to be in multi-task mode. Between the children, significant other, work, friends, family, over-committing, staying up to late, getting up early, etc. and we are clearly burning ourselves out. Is it possible that your body has gone into self-preservation mode and the notable shift in your mood is an indication to "pay attention" to *YOU*rself? Up until that point it is obvious you haven't slowed down enough to give your body what it needs. What if the same issue was happening with one of your child(ren)? What if you saw your child in burn-out stage and not taking care of themselves, first? What if they were always putting someone else's wants in front of their own and neglecting their personal well-being? What advice would you give them? What directives would you insist upon to help them feel better? What ways would you care for them? If you're like me then there's nothing you wouldn't do for your children and you would jump at the first opportunity to share with them anything you thought would help them out of their rut. Now let's flip that question on its back and let me ask you, why aren't you doing the same thing for yourself?

Is it possible that their self-neglect is a learned behavior, from you, and your child is now demonstrating it? Quite possibly. When we ignore, neglect and consistently put off our desires, needs and wants we are inevitably teaching them that who they are and what they want is not important. It sounds harsh but it is true. Those patterns ultimately lead to emotions of depression, low self-esteem, sadness and self-neglect. The good news is, we can all learn a new behavior. For instance, if your children are older you can share with them (and show them) how to slow down, learn to say no and take better care of themselves. If your children are still young you have the opportunity to start them off with a more balanced example of how to better care for themselves and their well-being. Take the time to give yourself the same tender loving care you would provide to your child. Care enough about YOU to find out what's going on with you….on a deeper level.

Here are 3 tips on how to identify and move beyond "what's really bothering you":

1) Clearly identify the issue. There are several ways to get clear but my best advice would be through meditation. Meditation is an opportunity for you to commune with your spirit. During this time you should cut yourself off from the "outside noise" of your life and find a quiet space to dwell on you (yes I said you!). According to National Cancer Institute as stated by WebMd, "….[meditation] It is a popular and proven form of stress relief and relaxing. Meditation seeks to focus your thoughts and gives you

more clarity and awareness.". Set your intention BEFORE you go into your meditation to accelerate awareness and find out what is longing for your attention. Meditation provides a great medium to expose whatever is 'bothering' you and provides you with an opportunity to reclaim your power over it.

Here are some sample questions you can ask while in meditation:

A) How can I take better care of myself, now?
B) Why am I feeling this way?
C) What should I be doing now?
D) What should I do next?
E) What is it that I really want?
F) What do I need to be more aware of?

2) Reclaim your power over it. Have you ever heard the old adage, "Knowledge is power"? There is absolute truth to this statement. What I know for sure is that when you know what issue you are facing—you will find yourself better able to equip and deal with it. In order to know what issue you are facing, you have to tell yourself the absolute, unadulterated truth. Admit to yourself your feelings. When you find yourself prepared to deal with whatever you are coming up against you feel empowered and more compelled to do whatever is necessary to resolve it.

3) Make a plan to come out of it. Now that you have identified what is REALLY bothering you…you have to muster up the courage and resolve to do WHATEVER it takes in order to be well.

Here are some solutions that I have used for the women in my program:

A.) Write down your goal. It helps you to visualize and makes you more accountable

B.) Say affirmations daily. Find, create, read and/or memorize affirmations that fortify you when times get tough; for when your neurological pathways begin to operate off of your memory (old paradigm) and default you into counter-productive thoughts and behavior. Affirmations are pivotal in changing your thought pattern.

C.) Learn how to say NO to others and YES to you. This may be somewhat difficult for you to do, in the beginning, especially if you are a people pleaser, however, it is imperative that you set boundaries around your time if you are to successfully reclaim your power.

While I am not making any proclamations for or against the Western medical philosophy, I stand by what has worked for me and many other women I have encountered and mentored over the years. I believe that if you try the above mentioned methodology you can successfully come out of your rut and reduce the number of recurrences going forward. Remember, every emotion is your body urging you to pay attention—calling you forth to a greater expression of who you came to be.

Putting first things first

I heard the most thorough explanation of this [putting first things first] from a book written by Mr. Stephen Covey called, Seven Habits of Highly Effective People (1). In sum, he urges the reader to distinguish between important activities and urgent activities and tend to them accordingly. Urgent means completion is critical and important means getting it done really matters. I had the awesome opportunity to become aware of how to prioritize these two, independent variables, and get both of my tasks completed without any stress.

In building my business I have committed to working Monday thru Friday for 5hours in the library. One Wednesday, I had a payment to make and it was in the front of my mind to take care of it and get it out of the way. My old thinking crept in and I was inclined to stop what I was doing, run to the bank pick up the money and drop off the payment. Then I had another thought. When is the payment due? What time is it now? What time does the bank close? What time does the establishment close? Will I have time to drop off the payment before they close? What commitment did I make to myself? What is my goal for the day? Is this decision in line with that goal/my value? Well, once I answered all of those questions the decision came very clear to me that I needed to honor my commitment, head over to the library and get to work. The payment was IMPORTANT but not URGENT. That was a pivotal moment for me because it represented a shift in my thought and a demonstration of more strategic thinking. How often have you made extensive plans and set lofty goals and when the slightest thing came up, you changed your plans and become de-railed. Sure, things change unexpectedly and we will always have to make adjustments but are you prioritizing properly by putting first things first? The right things? I certainly hope so.

As mothers we are ALWAYS juggling our "must-do's" and the children's "want to's". The question is, are we giving them the best example possible by analyzing the situation and making a decision based on putting first things first? Even if that means telling them *no* or *not right now*. Your goals and dreams are equally as important as your children's, your every decision must be based on that premise. Talk with your children. For example, if you are tending to an important task and your child wants your attention for a matter that is not urgent, there is no need to stop or re-arrange your priorities, that may warrant a conversation. Explain to them your decision, that you have considered their wants and when and how you will be able to assist them. You will be teaching your child patience, discipline, decision-making skills and a plethora of other life skills. Most importantly, you will be demonstrating what you are teaching and that is the best way to teach any lesson.

Here are 3 critical questions you should ask yourself before you take on any task:

1) Is this important or urgent?

2) Is this in line with my highest values/goals?

3) What adjustments will I need to make if I take on this task?

Use the above-mentioned questions going into any undertaking. What you will find is that some of the things you were going to do will be eliminated or re-prioritized and you will gain back one of your most valued assets----time.

Find an excuse to succeed

I get it, life is hard. There's so much to do and so little time to do it. There's never enough time in the day. You're exhausted. Yeah!Yeah!Yeah! Here's a dose of tough love, all of those are all excuses as to why you are not accomplishing your goal. Tell the truth---we all make time for what we WANT to do, somehow we find a way. Now put that on pause for a moment and shift your train of thought over to your children. Would you accept an excuse from them for say…..not completing their homework? Even if for some reason they did not complete it all that night---wouldn't you wake them up a little earlier in the morning so that they could have their assignment completed and turned in for full credit? For all practical purpose, sure you would. You would not allow anything that your child has to do or had done previously get in the way of them "handling their business". You are teaching them a philosophy to infuse in their standard of living---

"Let Nothing Stand In Your Way". If your children are like mine then they understand your philosophy and more times than not, they just hammer down and do it without excessive reminder (generally speaking, of course).

Now, let's un-pause the above mentioned situation---you. Why aren't you using this same philosophy and diligence when it comes to your life? Pursuing your dreams? Following your bliss? Goal achievement is not confined to the hours of nine to five and will often spill over into your "free" time. It takes sacrifice and determination to achieve the same values you are permeating in your children.

I remember when I wanted to complete my Master's Degree. My children were very young, ages 4, 6 and 8 at the time, and my husband was working and doing a lot of overtime. I had a determination to finish my degree within a certain time frame and I knew it would take sacrifice: sleep, "going out" and leisure time. I used to set my alarm for 1:00am in order to get just enough sleep to regain focus and energy and get back to work. I needed my family to be asleep so that I could have uninterrupted time to complete my readings, papers and assignments. I would sleep a few hours, after I got them off to school and work, then hop up to complete a few more hours until they returned home. Once they came in, I would feed them and then head over to the library where I could get a few moments, in block, where they were not calling me or "getting into something" and I could resume my studies. I would sit in the children's section (a lot more noise and traffic) so that they could play in the toddler area, for a few hours, until my husband would get off of work and pick them up. From there I would only have a couple of hours before the library closed, then I would have to interrupt my studies again to head home. It was hard. I was tired. I wanted to quit. But my will to succeed was GREATER than my excuse to quit, so I did what I had to do.

For my 9th year anniversary I went on a cruise. On the cruise, every morning before I started my day of leisure and romance I would get up, go work out and head down to the tables to study while waiting on my husband to join me. People told me to take a semester off, laughed and talked about me, but in July of 2010 I walked across stage with my 2nd Master's Degree --- 1 in Business Administration and the other in Human Resource Management. I had a mission to succeed and I was determined to accomplish my goal. I made a promise to myself and I had no intention of going back on my word. Equally important, my children were watching. I know that my children learn more by what I do than what I say and I wanted them to see me doing whatever was necessary to complete and accomplish what I set out to do. I know that when I am speaking with them about their responsibilities it provides more validity to my discussion and directives. It reinforces my point without having to add any emphasis. I can expect no more from them than I am willing to do for myself. So my 'excuse' to succeed is…."I don't feel like failing". I am the example that I want my children to be.

What's your excuse?

Doing nothing is doing something

So, you're sitting down watching television, the house is a wreck, you have errands to run, business to handle and cooking is not on your radar. GOOD! At this point, my recommendation would be to release the guilt of doing nothing. It's about time you sat down somewhere and relaxed and renewed. Why do we think the only time we deserve to sit down is when we are folding laundry, sick or sleep? There is always something to do and you will never be finish. Make peace with that.

With our busy schedules, hectic lives and varied roles we can all relate to biting off more than we can chew. Often times, we have so much on our plates that when our bodies finally do give out or we take a moment to sit down we are still talking about how much we need to do. We have got to stop! I became increasingly guilty of this after I had children. I thought the more I would do, in advance, the less I would have to do later. Here's the truth, children are as unpredictable as is life itself. We are never fully prepared for what's to come and rarely ever enjoy the moment we are in because we are always preparing for the next thing coming.

One of the biggest lessons you have the opportunity to learn, as parents, is that all your children really want is you. All of the clothes, toys, fixin's, gadgets, etc. are wonderful but more than anything else they want to feel that you are fully present and that you love them. For most moms, this is a paradigm shift. You have created much justification around your busy-ness that doing nothing is really hard to comprehend. Our efforts feel warranted because we believe it is for the betterment of our children; we believe we are doing the right thing. However, if you could believe, for a moment, that your child would be just fine if you took a day to watch television, go to the spa or stay in bed --and they would think no less of you-- would you do it? You have to realize that a lot of what you believe about parenting, children and yourself is made up. None of this information is necessarily true. You chose to believe everything you thought (or think) based upon the past and too often hold yourself hostage to this pre-dated standard. Of course, you want to use discernment and be wise in what you choose to believe and how you chose to act. Similarly, you want to be sure that you are completing regular self-audits of the thoughts you think, beliefs you hold and the behavior you act upon – they should be in service of you (your highest good). If they are not, STOP!

The quicker you realize that, the quicker you can decide to think and believe something different.

Decide to believe that taking care of yourself doesn't mean you are neglecting your children.

Decide to believe that giving yourself a day off, periodically, would mean being a better mother to your children and ultimately a better person to be around.

Decide to believe that showing your children how to take a day for yourself would be teaching them a form of self-love; to value their time and body.

When you *decide* to believe those things, it becomes easier and easier for you to enjoy your fun-filled day of doing nothing. When I made this shift, I began to, more thoroughly, enjoy the time I spent with my children because I felt rested, renewed and more energetic. Ultimately, I became more productive, my mood balanced out and now I have more clarity in my thoughts.

Going forward, I hope you happily plan your days off. As a matter of fact, you will probably notice that your children will literally encourage you to take days off. If they see that you are easily agitated or that your mood is somewhat off balanced, (often times) they will remind you that you need to take a day off. Everyone will soon realize that you doing "nothing" is actually doing something for the whole family.

Do you take time just for you?
Do you feel guilty when you are doing nothing?

We all deserve some down time—no matter how busy we are. We must honor our bodies if we want it to remain healthy, vital and cogent. Below I have outlined some of the best practices in planning your MVIP day (Mommy's Very Important Personal Day).

Tips on planning your down time:

1) Communicate your intentions with your (immediate) family members. Let them know you will not be available and that means for ANYTHING. This is most effective when you give them no more than a 24hr notice.

2) Don't answer the phone. Anything short of an emergency can wait. You have caller

ID, text and voicemail---if it's that important they'll leave a message.

3) Be in the moment. Be fully present in your time off (and always) and do only what you want.

4) Enjoy. Don't waste your down time feeling guilty.

Relax on purpose!

So, you didn't reach your goal

You have your plans all laid out. You have created a schedule with all considerations taken into account. You have visualized. You have meditated. You have prayed. You have put forth the effort. You are all prepared to complete your mission. Unfortunately, you fail. For some reason, someone didn't do what they were supposed to do and that prohibited you from completing what you needed to complete; that snowballed into you missing a deadline; from that you were un-informed on how to complete.....WHEW! Take a breath, stop blaming and let it go!

As angry as you are about 'not hitting your mark' that still won't change the outcome. Not only will it not change the outcome, you are actually creating physiological problems in your body that are completely avoidable (elevated heartbeat, increased blood pressure, anxiety, etc.). As moms, sometimes we can be too hard on ourselves. For some reason we don't allow ourselves the same courtesy and forgiveness that we offer our girlfriends, family members and our children when they make a *mis*-take. Who do we think we are? A super-human that transcends error? Let's stop torturing our-selves. When you begin to be-little and berate yourself you only sink further into the emotion of failure and loss and wind up moving yourself further away from a viable solution to rectify the issue. Think about when your children fail to achieve a laid out goal that they had for themselves. What is one of the first things that you tell them? It may sound something like this, "it's okay sweetheart, just try harder next time....". That statement does three things that you may not have even taken a moment to become aware of:

1) It validates the child's feelings. You are addressing the fact that there has been a breakdown between the desire and the

outcome. It lets the child know that you care about how they feel and the effect it had on them.

2) It stimulates the child's brain into a solution-oriented frame of mind. Maybe trying harder isn't the solution---but it will provoke more expansive thinking to figure out what is.

3) Safe space is created. You have created a 'space' for that child to feel safe with their emotions and redeem their self-esteem.

How much better would you feel about yourself if you were nurtured in that same way? Can you consider giving that to yourself in order to empower your goals? It's far more productive to shift your emotions to acceptance verses being overly-critical.

To be clear, I am not saying that you should be cavalier with your goals or any expectation you set for yourself. I do believe that a balanced approach to personal accountability is appropriate if you want to move ahead with any endeavor and accomplish your goals. However, too much of anything is not a good thing. Therefore, wallowing in self-pity, harsh criticism and agitation will only give you more of the same thing and likely reduce your desire to make another effort. Give yourself the opportunity to do better. See your so-called failures as lessons. Decide that you are going to maintain your positive attitude about the outcome whether you reach the desired goal or not. Believe it or not, your success starts with your attitude. Think about what Thomas Edison, credited for inventing the light bulb, said when asked about all of his failures in the creation of the light bulb. He said, "… I have not failed, I have just found 10,000 ways that don't work." You are meant to thrive and have everything that you want and more. Don't waste your time complaining about what didn't work, instead use the lesson you learned to help catapult you forward.

If for some reason you create a plan and it doesn't work, there is a way to move out of the disappointment of that moment and more quickly create the desired outcome. Here are 4 quick tips to help you create a win-win situation:

1) Make a decision that it's ok. Don't be harsh on yourself. Remember, everyone makes mistakes and you are not exempt.

2) Make a new agreement with yourself. If it didn't work out on the schedule you planned, set a new date. Take into consideration all that you have learned from the original plan and the goal you have in mind and create a new "goal achievement" date.

3) Apologize. Acknowledge whomever was directly involved with the outcome of your goal completion, it's important to recognize your error. This expresses ownership and a willingness to take full responsibility for the disparity between the desire and the outcome

4) Set a new expectation with all parties involved. If there is any type of collaboration with others and they will be affected by the outcome then it is important to share your new expectations for yourself. It's a way that others can support you in being accountable to your new set of goals.

Don't let complaining and blaming rob you of your time and goals.

Time Management: There is no such thing

Here's the truth, you can't manage time. We are all given the same amount of seconds, minutes and hours in a day. All we can do is manage the task around that time in order to be most effective and efficient to get the most done. When you begin to manage your task properly, you will notice some things begin to disappear from your to-do list. You will set out to complete things that will support you in completing your goal and delete anything that is not congruent. Here's another truth, you still won't get it *all* done, all the time, make peace with that.

I know you have great expectations for yourself and big things you want to accomplish. However, if you step back and take a look at what you have done so far….you will notice that you are, likely, doing better than you thought and much closer to your goal than you even noticed. I understand, almost doesn't count….but baby steps do and what I know for sure is that if you allow yourself to pay attention to your successes it fuels your motivation and pushes you further. It's a mental thing, everything starts in the mind. And if you can train your mind to see the positive, believe it's possible and persevere, your brain will begin to find/create ways for you to accomplish what you once thought you couldn't. Inevitably giving you clear direction on what task you need to prioritize with the time you are given.

Here's the caveat, when you being to master your task management schedule, you must be prepared to release some things. When you are operating in what is called your "Zone of Genius" (as described by Gay Hendricks in the book, "The Big Leap") things, people and events that are not operating in your same vibrational frequency will be removed from your experience. Find comfort in knowing that everything you are separating yourself from is counter-productive to your goal, therefore, not making the most efficient use of your time. It must be released. At first, this is very uncomfortable because there is no bias in what or whom will be removed. It could be a friend, relative or even a spouse. In short, just get comfortable being uncomfortable.

It doesn't mean that all ties will be severed from this person, eternally. It simply means that at this time and for this purpose (that you have claimed) it would not be in your highest interest to interact with the person. When you resist this natural order and desire to hold on to what is comfortable, it makes this shift even more difficult. It not only separates you further from your goal but it is a "waste" your time. The Universe is responding to your request and is always acting in your favor, trust the process.

When you are free from excess people, events and places, you are made available to complete the things you have set out to accomplish, and then you are able to use your time on people and the things that are in service of supporting your goals. Open yourself up to the possibility of doing things differently than you have ever done before. When you do this, it will seem as though you have been given more time than others, or that you have re-gained time once lost. Actually, you are just using the time you have been given more wisely.

As it relates to our children, depending on what age they are or the situation at hand, we may not be able to re-arrange the task of tending to what is needed. It may very well be that you have to stop what you are doing in order to address whatever issues may arise. Take a breath, it's okay. There are several ways to deal with it:

1) Stop what you are doing, momentarily, rectify the issue then return to your task

2) Acknowledge the issue and then explain to your child that you are 'working' and give them a time when you will be free

3) Bring the child(ren) where you are and give them an activity to complete/enjoy while you resume your task

The key is to set parameters around your time.

Many of the reasons why your time is mis-handled is that you are not establishing your goals first. Once you establish the goal, you will gain more clarity on the importance of eliminating people and things that are not in support of your goal. Additionally, you will learn that setting parameters around your time is essential to your achievement. You are worthy of every goal you set and you have all the time you need to complete it. Optimize your time by managing your task.

Keep Pushing

We all have times where we are ready to throw in the towel. The children are acting crazy, you burned the dinner, your spouse is on your last nerves, you're having a bad hair day and the laundry is just about as tall as you are. Good grief! Girlfriend, we have all been there and I am here to tell you---you can make it.

When life piles up and you feel like you're drowning, STOP. Take a deep breath and ask yourself, what do I value the most? Now, go and do that thing first. Do it without thinking that you 'should' be doing something else. Be fully present in the moment YOU have chosen. Those other things will be there when you get to them and if they are not—trust that it's what's best and move on. You have to save your energy for the things you can control. You have so much that you want for yourself, your children and your family so do not dawdle away the little time you have with meager thoughts of what *could have* been done.

Now that we've got that out of the way, let's discuss what to do when you have prioritized everything, let go of others and you still feel that you want to throw in the towel. Keep pushing! The energy that you use for times when you don't feel like going any further will make it easier for you to go even further the next time. I often tell my children and my mentees that the only difference between what you have and what you want is perseverance. You've got to do it when you don't feel like it. That is the secret formula; that is the secret sauce. I think about times when I didn't feel like writing my book. I really had some valid reasons (in my head) as to why I couldn't do it. My children's activities, I didn't feel well, lunch with girlfriends, date night with hubby, tired, traveling, overtime, etc. but in reality none of that mattered to my bottom line. I had a goal and I needed to do whatever it took to get it done. I had to honor my commitment to *myself* and come up with a plan to get it done.

While in school, there were many instances where I had to set my alarm for one or two o'clock in the morning just so that I could get some alone time to reach the goal I had for myself. Did I like it? Truthfully, nope! However, my commitment to myself was greater than my desire to quit so I refused to let ANYTHING or ANYONE stand in the way of me accomplishing my goals.

If you have given up on yourself in the past, don't fret. Every day presents a new opportunity to try again and I want to see you succeed.

Here are some ways to overcome over-whelm and keep pushing:

1) Create a list of goals – Writing down your goals will help you to keep them in the forefront of your mind. Metaphysics' believe that writing things down changes our

vibration (our energy) and increases the likelihood that it will get done.

2) Everyday, at least 7 times per day, read your goals. In the spiritual realm, it is believed that seven represents completion/creation and the relationship between the divine and the human. Additionally, repetition keeps the goals in the foremost thoughts of your mind, thus helping you guide your decisions to support your goals.

3) Everyday listen to something positive or inspirational – This will help you when those old paradigms and self-sabotaging habits creep in. We all have a voice inside of us that tells us we can't do it and gives us reasons why. When you feed your mind, daily, with motivational information and the negative voices or people surface, you will have the tools to combat those thoughts/people and are free to push forward.

Getting Unstuck

This has to be one of the hardest things in the world to do. You know what you need to do. You have every intention of doing it. You know you need to do it in order to complete/fulfill your goal. Why aren't you doing it? The simple truth is: you're stuck! You find yourself engaging in busy work (anything that can wait) or creating a situation in order to justify why you are not doing what you KNOW you should. There is no scientific reason behind this---it's all a part of human nature. However, that does not excuse you from taking the necessary steps to get you back on task. Where I'm from we called it 'stalling". That's a colloquial term that means 'taking a long time to do something'. Please note, there is nothing wrong with you and you have everything you need to get started right now; you are just plain ol' stalling---welcome to the club. Don't worry, this is the no judgment zone, all

I want to do is help you to identify the issue and work through it. Whew! Now that we have that off of our chest, let's look at some of the reasons why we tend to stall and wind up stuck.

For all intents and purposes we have a clear understanding of what we want to do. We may not know how to get it done, but we are pretty clear on what we want and the outcome we are looking to yield. For example, I knew I wanted to motivate moms using multiple platforms/various mediums that allowed me to travel all over the world empowering them with the tools they needed to honor their dreams and be great women and mothers. I had no clue how to reach the masses. How I would get my name out? What platform/medium options do I have? Who would teach me the business? What tools/resources would I need, etc.? Of course, with all of my hopes and dreams percolating in my mind and beckoning me forward, I had to face my current reality. I still had to help with homework, do laundry, dishes, drop off/pick up, practice, games, playdates, hangout, etc. life didn't provide me with any time-outs to sort out or work my plan. So as you can imagine I was feeling overwhelmed and fearful.

There was so much I didn't know and what I did know, I had no clear path on how to manifest. There were times when all I could do was climb in the bed and watch television. I didn't know what to do and because of that I felt that I should do --- nothing. Have you ever felt that way? Have you ever done that? The only thing that happens when you stall out of your responsibilities is that you lose time, momentum and confidence. When you are not using time wisely...it gives you unspoken permission to continue engaging in non-productive activity. When I was growing up my mom used to call it being idol. Whenever you are idol, it leaves room for old paradigms to creep in and talk you out of your mission.

Most often, when you have something you want to do, it comes with a burst of energy, ideas and actions. Ideally, you act on those energies and begin to engage others with questions, information and activities you are doing towards your goal. Then, you get an answer you don't like, or come to a point when you don't know something or hit a road block and you begin to retreat. You begin to slow what was once a sprint into a menial walk. Once you begin to do that you start to lose confidence. You begin to believe that as a result of what is happening with you, right now, reaching your dream is not possible. So you begin to engage in what I call avoidance behaviors that come in the disguise of being stuck.

If you are honest with yourself, you have likely avoided taking the next step for at least one of the following five reasons:

1. Fear
2. Overwhelmed

3. Uncertainty

4. Procrastination

5. Lazy

There is an interconnectedness with the above-mentioned and if allowed it can spiral out of control.

Make a different decision.

How to get unstuck:

1) Deliberately take a day off from the thing you are looking to complete. Physically step away from *doing* anything to/towards it. Don't think about it, do anything towards it nor discuss it with anyone. Stepping away from something and giving your mind a chance to re-group often brings about new ideas and a different perspective.

2) Meditate/Contemplate for a full 24 hours. Mentally, use the power of your mind to imagine yourself completing it, the resources you need showing up, the

difference it would make in your life, etc. When you do this it super-charges your energy/motivation and refocuses intention.

3) Do at least one thing, every day, toward the completion of your ultimate goal. This gives you a sense of accomplishment and forward momentum.

You have the power within you, right now, to move from where you are to where you want to be. You are a winner!

Recommitment

So, you're feeling good about the vision you have for your life and you are all ready to go full speed ahead. You have plans that surround your vision. You have set goals to help you accomplish the vision. The day comes that you are intended to get started aaannnddddd......... YOU DON'T. Has this ever happened to you? Do you get started when you intended and somewhere along the road you have a segment of time where you didn't accomplish anything you have laid out in your plans? If this has ever happened to you then it's likely you have experienced one (or many) of these feelings:

- disappointment
- frustration
- anger
- guilt
- confusion

Those are all normal feelings and organic emotions when you fail to do something you set out to accomplish. What happened? How did you get to this point?

The reality of life is that everything comes in waves. From inspiration to devastation—we will all be visited by each of these at some point. You don't always get to choose which emotion will strike, however, you do get to choose how you will handle what comes your way. The way you handle a situation can leave you feeling empowered or victimized and you get to decide which one it will be. Isn't it exciting to know that you have a choice in how you feel? Isn't it liberating to know that you are the authority over your feelings?

Let's say you have a goal of completing the laundry on a certain day. You have it fixed in your mind and know that if you complete it on that certain day that it will free you up to do something else later. Your family's clothes that they need for the week will be all refreshed and that is one more thing you can take off of your to-do list. However, life happened and you don't feel well or you didn't finish another project you had intentions of completing before now. Or, something else popped up that took priority over the goal and totally cancelled all other plans for the day. Or, the day came and you...just...didn't...feel like it! Take a deep breath, I know that last one took you for a loop.

So often we look for grand reasons as to why we didn't do something and sometimes we just don't feel like it--- and that's the reason why.

The real objective is to get pass the mis-step and make a new agreement with yourself. In many instances, it's not that big of a deal, all you have to do is recommit to doing better next time. Lighten up.

Here are 4 ways to honor your experience and move beyond it:

1) Feel what you are feeling. You have a right to your feelings. Ignoring them or wishing that they were different is to dishonor your authenticity. The feelings that you are experiencing came to teach you something— to show you a way that things can be done differently for the future. Take the time to experience the feeling and figure out what it came to teach you.

2) Be gentle with yourself. Remember, nobody's perfect and beating yourself up over this issue will only compound the problem. Take the opportunity to examine the behavior surrounding the incident and why you didn't follow through.

3) Write down what you did instead. This will help you to identify patterns and possible

self-sabotaging behaviors, to avoid, for future reference.

4) Recommit. This is always an option. Make a conscious decision to release the date that you intended to complete the task. Don't "should" all over yourself (I should have done this, I should have completed that, etc.). Making a new commitment allows you to acknowledge your prior agreement (with yourself), holds you accountable (exposing that you did indeed miss the mark) and establishes a new goal for you to make a commitment.

Remember, shame is the lowest vibration of emotion and distracts positive momentum. Instead, use your energy to glean from the incident your opportunity to do better next time. Release any attachment to what you thought it should have looked like and recommit to doing whatever is necessary to meet the goal.

Ask for help

For centuries history has defined the dominant role of women to be submissive, homemakers and baby bearing beauties. While I am not against that stereotype (to each their own), I don't believe that women who do not fit within that framework or are some sort of variation outside of it should have to "fight" or defend themselves in order to be their authentic selves. We should all have the luxury of our choice in being who we came to this planet to be as a wife, mother, etc. However, so often I find that women, especially mothers, are over compensating in their role in effort to combat any preconceived notions that others may have of them. For example, I have a strong dislike for cooking. I have known that since I was a little girl. I was the child that every time my mother would try and teach me about cooking or have me assist her in the kitchen, I would come up with a random illness or pain and that allowed me leave the room. I would find any excuse under the sun to get out of learning/helping. When I became an adult and married my husband the same dislike for cooking held true. However, because of the unwritten rules of society I thought in order for me to be seen as a "good wife/mother" I needed to be in the kitchen preparing the meals. As a matter of fact, I was a stay at home mom (11years) so I surely thought I had *better* learn how to cook in order to 'earn' and maintain my right to stay at home. It was a warped sense of thinking, I know, but at the time, I didn't even realize that I held this subconscious belief and how much it guided my decisions. Day after day I would toil, sweat and be-labor over meals that looked so simple and easy for my mother (and others) to cook, yet, it took me literally all day to make. I was not happy. Then one day it dawned on me, "stop trying to cook, you don't like it and you don't know how". It can be very liberating to admit, to yourself, your truth without considering the feelings of anyone else.

Not only did I admit it to myself but I told my husband, friends, family and anyone else that would listen when the conversation came up. I knew that I was ok with it when I didn't care (one bit) about the opinion of others. The biggest revelation for me was my husband's reaction; not only was he supportive of my admission but he gladly took over the meal preparation. I had no idea he had such a gift of cooking delicious meals and could throw down in the kitchen (yummy!).

I share this with you because in a round-about-way this was my way of asking for help. I could have avoided (literally) years of frustration and wasted time if I would have simply asked for help. Instead, I let my ego and the opinion of others dictate the way I functioned within my own household. Now as a mentor, I see the same thing happening with other women I work with in my program. You don't even realize that you are holding yourself hostage to the dysfunction of your own beliefs. You are walking through life unconscious of the fact that your frustration, discomfort and anger could be lessened if you simply asked for what you wanted.

Do yourself a favor, ask for help. Don't wait until you are exhausted, frustrated and at your wits end. I am certain that more people than you actually realize would take pleasure in helping you in whatever way they are able.

Additionally, I want you to realize that asking for help doesn't make you weak or any less of the awesome mother and person you are. Contrarily, it establishes you as a leader. You will become a mother who knows that you didn't come here to be everything to everybody and that you can ask for help, at any time. You realize that self-care *IS* noble and that taking care of yourself, first, enables you to take better care of your family and be of service to the world.

Lessen your frustration with three simple steps:

1) Admit to yourself that you need help. There is no shame in needing help. It doesn't make you weak or any less of a woman; it actually makes you stronger, better and wiser.

2) Find someone who is willing to help you with your situation. The African proverb, "...it takes a village" is applicable to more than just raising the children. Leverage your community.

3) Ask for help. Once you identify your needs and have found someone who you trust to carry out your request, ask. You aren't afraid of the judgment of others because you reach out for help in areas that traditionally women are expected to handle. You set the standards you live by, and by doing that, you empower others to do the same.

You are your own best advocate!

You *ARE* More Than Their Mother

I honor where you are right now on your journey. Your decision to read this book is proof that you want to experience more.

You are smart, you are driven, you are creative and you are loving. The totality of your being cannot be compromised for your singular role as mother. You cannot become less than who you are. You're More Than Their Mother™

Now it's time to make a decision. Will you decide to stop blaming others and the past as to why you are not where you want to be? Are you ready to stop using motherhood as an excuse for you not going after the dreams? You hold the key, you have the power. It all starts with your decision to be different.

The main goal of this book is to let you know that you are not alone. I designed this Book, The S.O.A.R Mentoring Program, Presentations and everything else to let you know that there is support --- I get it.

If you are interested in joining like-minded women who have decided to RE-claim the dreams they once had and live the life they have always imagined, then I would love to work with you.

Go to the website:

www.youremorethantheirmother.com

and learn more about the S.O.A.R. Mentoring Program. If it speaks to you, then fill out the application and let's get started!

It's time to move beyond everyone else's expectations of who you ought to be and become the woman YOU thought that you could be.

Acknowledgments

I have so much to be grateful for and so many people to thank. First, I want to thank my wonderful husband, Gerald "Schnookums" Dorsey (YES! that's my nickname for him *smile*). Gerald you have been my Number 1 fan, friend and avid supporter since we began dating at the tender age of sixteen. You mean the world to me and it's my pleasure being your wife.

To my dynamic daughters, Mahogany, Ashia and Mizan. You all came here to teach me how to become a better me through my loving you.

Mahogany, your attention to detail and your gentle spirit has taught me to slow down and not take things personally. It is all working out in my favor!

Ashia, your tenacity and ambition has taught me that perseverance is the only thing standing between what I want and what I have. I can do anything!

Mizan, your strong-will and determination has taught me to eliminate anything that is not in support of my goals. I no longer consider the opinion of others when reaching my decision – I now know that as long as I am in integrity with myself, I can't offend anyone else. I am a Woman of Power!

Thank you daughters for being exactly who you are and the answer to my prayers. I love you girls!

To my wonderful parents, Willie and Shirley Jones. Words cannot express what your love and belief in me has meant. The strength I have comes from the support you have given to me, all of my life, and I appreciate your boundless love. To my siblings, Alvin Jones and Kimberly Jones-Smith, thank you for looking out for your baby sister -- even when I only wanted to be the baby when it was convenient for me. You allowed me to be myself.

To both of my nephews, all of my aunts, uncles, cousins, in-laws, friends and my grandmother, you all have been my biggest cheerleaders! Thank you for the emotional, spiritual and personal guidance. There is no way I could have made it this far without you. I love you all, a lot!

Last, but certainly not least, my mentors – all of them. You all have played a role in me writing this book and stepping into my greatness. Thank you for encouraging me to be my authentic self. Because of you, I stopped standing in my potential and moved to my now and for that I am grateful.

Reference Page

Web MD. (2015, December 27). Health and Balance: Meditation Directory. Retrieved from: http://www.webmd.com/balance/meditation-directory

Covey, Stephen R. The 7 Habits of Highly Effective People: Powerful Lessons in Personal Change. New York: Free, 2004

PhD. Hendricks, Gay. The Big Leap: Conquer Your Hidden Fear and Take Life to the Next Level. Harper College: 2010

Made in the USA
Columbia, SC
26 February 2020